GREAT RAILWAY STATIONS
OF EUROPE

To Amy from Mike

Happy Birthday 1990

GREAT RAILWAY STATIONS ❧ OF EUROPE ❧

Text by Marcus Binney   ·   Photographs by Manfred Hamm   ·   Notes by Axel Foehl

with 107 illustrations, 50 in color

THAMES AND HUDSON

©1984 Nicolaische Verlagsbuchhandlung, Berlin
English text ©1984 Thames and Hudson Ltd, London

First published in the USA in 1985 by Thames and Hudson Inc., 500 Fifth Avenue,
New York, New York 10110

Reprinted 1985

Library of Congress Catalog Card Number 84-51234

Printed and bound in West Germany

CONTENTS

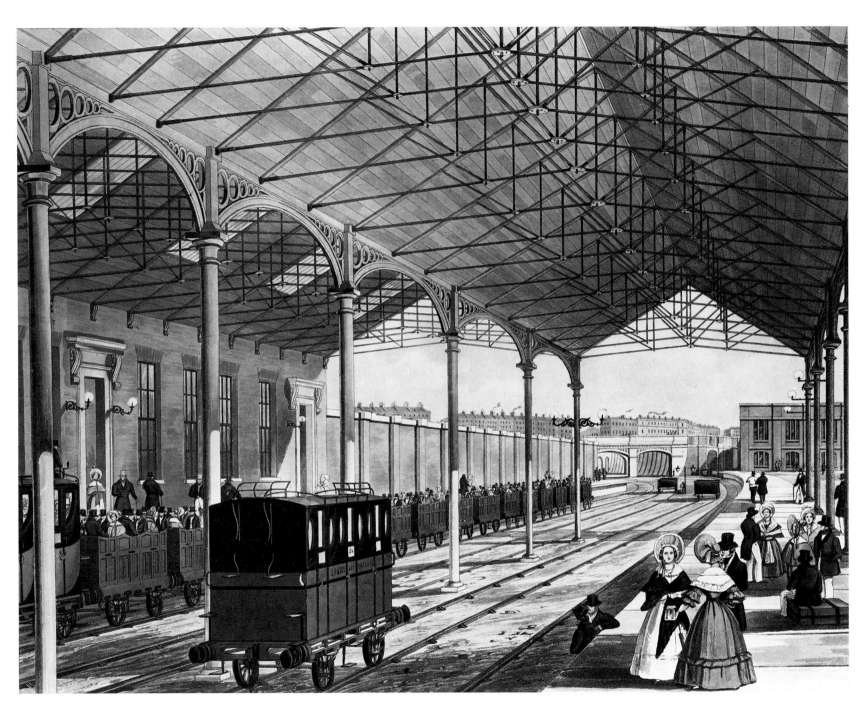

Euston Station in London was the first of the great European termini. This view shows it in 1837, soon after its opening. The train on the left consists mostly of open third-class carriages. Beyond them two monumental doorways lead to the palatial booking-hall, whose rich classical architecture contrasted with the functional iron and glass of the train-shed.

INTRODUCTION

The design of railway stations in the 19th century, like that of airports today, evoked strong feelings: 'One of the great architectural infamies of our century', Jacob Burckhardt wrote of the Gare du Nord in 1897. Ruskin, as might be expected, also expressed his views forcefully: 'Better bury gold in the embankments than put it in ornaments on the stations . . . Railroad architecture has, or would have, a dignity of its own, if it were only left to its work. You would not put rings on the fingers of a smith at his anvil.'

In the great days of railways, cities took pride in the architecture of their railway termini; guidebooks described and lauded them. Murray's *Handbook to London* in 1879 says of the London termini that many 'deserve to be visited as architectural and engineering wonders. Especially worthy of note are the Midland, Great Northern and Great Western Terminals' – better known today as St Pancras, King's Cross and Paddington. Sampson's *Guide to York*, published in 1893, boasts that the city's station is the 'largest station in the United Kingdom and therefore we suppose in the world'.

Once across the Alps, Mark Twain in his *Pleasure Trip to the Continent* (1871) admired the railway stations 'more than Italy's hundred galleries of priceless art treasures . . . In the turnpikes, the railways, the depôts, and the new boulevards of uniform houses in Florence and other cities here, I see the genius of Louis Napoleon'.

In this century the architecture of railway stations finds virtually no mention in guidebooks – Baedeker, Muirhead, Blue Guides and *Guides Bleus* list the main termini in every city but rarely pass comment on them, and even as 19th-century architecture emerges from prolonged eclipse, the situation is only now beginning to change, prompted by a growing literature on railway architecture and travel, and exhibitions such as the Centre Georges Pompidou's *Le Temps des Gares*, which opened in Paris in 1978 and has since been shown all over Europe.

Yet through much of this century railway stations have been a powerful attraction, especially to the young. Rudolf Nureyev, in his *Autobiography* published in 1962 when he was just twenty-four, recalled how when a boy he would go to a hill above the Railway Station at Ufa, the town where he grew up. 'I would sit there motionless for hours, watching. For several years of my life I think I went there every day, simply watching the trains slowly starting and getting up speed. I loved the sensation of being driven somewhere else by those wheels. I was more attached to that railway station than to school or even to home.' Later, in Leningrad, he would go to the station when creating a role in a new ballet and watch until he felt the movement become 'part of me and I part of the train'.

Those who came to stations simply to watch and look were not always so popular with the station-master and his staff. E.B. Ivatts, goods manager of the Midland Great Western Railway, complained of this in his *Railway Management at Stations* (I quote from the fourth edition of 1904): 'The idlers appear to have increased, as a railway station is now frequented to obtain a little excitement, to see the people, to hear the news and to read the titles of the new novels at the bookstalls. Undoubtedly the bookstalls have largely increased the idlers'.

Passenger stations are composed of two main elements: first the platforms and tracks, and secondly the booking hall and other facilities, such as waiting rooms, buffets, restaurants and shops. In most of the great terminals illustrated in this book, passenger facilities and platforms are on a single level, and passengers move unconsciously and freely from booking hall to train-shed. But around the turn of the 19th century a new arrangement developed, particularly in North America. This created a complete division between the station building with a large concourse, and the platforms. In many such stations the concourse is actually above the platforms, and serves as a giant footbridge across them, complete with booking offices, shops and restaurants. In Britain, however, this system never became established, partly because most of the great termini were already built, partly because the coal used by locomotives was less smoky than in North America, and there was less reason to separate the trains from the waiting area.

The arrangements for passengers varied considerably from one European country to another. Baedeker's *Paris and Environs* (1907) complains of the Paris stations: 'Before starting, travellers are generally cooped up in the close and dusty waiting rooms, and are not admitted to the platform until the train is ready to receive them.' According to Ivatts, the French system may have been modelled on the early practice of the Great Western Railway where, 'on a departure platform there were three railed-in spaces for first, second and third class passengers, and the passengers after taking their tickets were ushered into these spaces which the public sarcastically styled pens.' When the train was ready (or at an intermediate station, when it arrived) the passengers were let out from the pens onto the platforms. At the large stations in Paris, Ivatts observed, passengers, having obtained their tickets, were ushered down a long passage from which opened three saloons or waiting rooms for first, second and third class passengers. These rooms were situated along the platforms but 'the passengers are completely boxed-up in them and cannot even see or go to the platforms.' When the train was ready, sliding doors opened – first class passengers being allowed a minute's start on the others. In the United States and Canada a similar system operated with passengers waiting inside the main station building rather than on the platform. But 'the British biped', Ivatts noted, 'likes to meander up and down a railway platform [and] would raise a loud outcry if curtailed of his present liberty to do so'.

This praise of open platforms is carried a stage further in Perdonnet and Polonceau's *Nouveau Portefeuille des Chemins de Fer* (1843-46). The large platforms, they wrote, 'are really a great and beautiful spectacle which gives a just idea of the power and the liberalism of the companies which have given their countries these marvellous instruments of travel. The travellers, entering the stations freely at any hour, familiarize themselves with the engines. In admiring them they cease to fear them, and it is thus that railways become popular.' By this line of argument, handsome station buildings and great train-sheds had a deliberate commercial intent in winning custom for the railways. Put travellers in waiting rooms, they concluded, 'and companies seem to doubt their confidence'.

Yet confinement in waiting rooms continued in many parts of Europe, and the quality of facilities for different classes of passenger regularly receives comment in guidebooks. The 1876 edition of Murray's *Handbook for Holland and Belgium* complains chauvinistically of the discomforts the Belgium system produced, particularly at minor stations. 'There is frequently no separation in the waiting rooms between the passengers of different classes, and the traveller, locked in until the moment when his train arrives, must often endure the society of Belgian boors.'

In Germany waiting rooms were provided for no less than four classes of passenger. In Britain, Perdonnet and Polenceau observed, the first class waiting room was always separate, but those for the second and third classes were sometimes combined. In the 1866 edition of their *Portefeuille* they note a different distinction at the Gare du Nord in Paris: the waiting rooms for suburban trains were far from the platforms and made a long walk inevitable, but those for long-distance travellers were much closer to the trains.

Cassell's *Railway Guides*, each covering one of the main British Railway Companies, provide a fascinating insight into the facilities available for passengers. At some stations, like Paddington and King's Cross, the principal facilities were placed on one side beside the main departure platform. Of King's Cross *The Great Northern Railway Guide* (1912 edition) says: 'The main line departure platform is supplied with refreshment-rooms, well-appointed breakfast, luncheon and dining rooms, and a charmingly appointed tea-room.' The contemporary Cassell's *Midland Railway Guide* boasts: 'At all Midland Refreshment Rooms a glass of filtered water can always be obtained free of charge'. Special emphasis was placed on facilities for ladies – and not only the separate ladies' waiting room which is still a common feature at large stations today. Joannes' *Guide de Grande Bretagne et Irlande* in 1865 states that 'at the buffets in the large stations ladies will find staff of their own sex to wait on them'.

In Scandinavia, self-service came early. Baedeker's *Norway, Sweden and Denmark* in 1912, comments on the good restaurants at large stations. 'Passengers help themselves and pay on entering and leaving.' Many trains, it adds, stopped for fifteen to twenty minutes at certain stations for meals. O'Shea's *Guide to Spain and Portugal* in 1905, observes that 'the station buffets as a rule are good and not extortionate, and meal-times are always arranged for the itinerary'.

Before restaurant cars were introduced it was customary for trains to stop at larger stations and allow passengers to disembark for a meal. Mark Twain wrote rapturously about the arrangements in France compared with his native America. 'But the happiest regulation in French railway government is – thirty minutes for dinner! No five minute bolting of flabby rolls, muddy coffee, questionable eggs, gutta percha beef . . . No, we sat calmly down – it was in old Dijon . . . and poured out rich Burgundian wines and munched calmly through a long table d'hôte bill of fare, snail patties, delicious fruits and all.'

In Switzerland, station restaurants have long been acknowledged as good and reliable places to eat in almost every town, but in other countries too the best station restaurants have always attracted strong local patronage. Baedeker's *Northern Italy* (1936) notes that the restaurant of the Stazione Centrale in Turin is much frequented by the inhabitants. Today in the Michelin guide to France the Buffet Gare at Arras is the only restaurant in the town to receive a rosette. At the Charing Cross Hotel in London, British Rail have proudly renamed the hotel restaurant 'The Sir John Betjeman' – to return the complement Betjeman paid in his *London's Historic Railway Stations* (1972). 'The dining room', he wrote, 'except for that at the Ritz, is the most finely appointed hotel dining room in London.'

Far excelling the dining room at Charing Cross, the restaurant at the Ritz, and even the Casino at Monte Carlo is the spectacular restaurant at the Gare de Lyon in Paris, today known as 'Le Train Bleu'. The Gare de Lyon, like the Gare d'Orsay was constructed on the eve of the *Exposition universelle* of 1900. The buffet completed in 1901 occupies the first floor of the main station building and consists of two main salons as richly decorated with frescoes and stucco as the great Renaissance galleries at Fontainebleau, though here the idiom is *fin de siècle* at its most voluptuous.

John Pendleton in his two volume evocation *Our Railways*, published in 1894, however, complained that the early bird did not get the most delicious worm, but rather 'an overnight sandwich' curled at the corners which 'had been in a glass prison for eight hours at least'. The writer C.S. Lewis, one reviewer has recalled, had a still stranger phobia. Until his late marriage, he had grave doubts about pork pies. They were aphrodisiac, he said, and inadvisable for a bachelor, especially in railway buffets.

Most station buffets supplied packed lunches. Baedeker's *Northern Italy* in 1930 mentions luncheons in paper bags (*cestini*) – 7½-15 lire for cold meat, bread and wine. *The Midland Railway Guide* advised patrons that 'telegrams will be sent free of charge' to principal stations 'ordering luncheons, dinner, trays of tea, or other refreshments, on notice being given to the guard of the train, or to the station master or other railway official'.

The most lavish restaurants were of course to be found in the great railway hotels which rose by many of the main termini. *The Midland Railway Guide* naturally waxed proudly on Sir George Gilbert Scott's magnificent hotel at St Pancras: 'The late George Augustus Sala said the Midland Hotel was "destined to be one of the most prosperous in the Empire", a singularly sanguine forecast . . . but amply verified, chiefly thanks to Mr William Towle, Manager of Midland Hotels and Refreshment Rooms.'

The Midland Hotel standing on a massive, private, raised terrace above Euston Road still looks like a grand hotel in a seaside or mountain resort. It was designed, according to *The Midland Guide* 'to afford the best features of the English, the American and the Continental systems'. Particular emphasis was placed on the 'noiseless interior', which 'by specially designed screens is shielded from the bustle of the adjoining station'. By this time the hotel boasted a 'new smoking lounge for ladies and gentlemen on the first floor' as well as prettily arranged sitting rooms with bedrooms *en suite*.

A few pages further on, the new Midland Hotel (now no more) opposite Central Station in Manchester is proclaimed as 'one of the most palatial of such structures to be found in Europe' with a 'magnificent octagon court of coloured marble, richly decorated and surmounted by an ornamented dome. A beautiful garden framed by trellis work and finished with flower beds of green faience' was laid out below. Furnishings and decorations were by the distinguished Lancashire firm of Waring and Gillow, aided by Marsh, Jones, Cribb & Co. At Leeds an advertisement in *The Great Northern Railway Guide* of 1912 announced that the Great Northern Hotel had recently been redecorated and refurbished by Maple & Co., of London and Paris. The Great Eastern Hotel at Liverpool Street Station, according to Cassell's *Great Eastern Railway Guide* (1892), hired rooms for 'wedding breakfasts, consultations, arbitrations, masonic lodges' – and the lodges continue to meet there today in a splendid room with sumptuous Rococo revival plasterwork.

After mentioning the station buffets in Belgium, Murray's 1876 *Handbook* goes on to praise 'the dressing-rooms (*cabinets de toilettes*)' which are 'a great comfort and convenience for passengers'. Latrines and urinoirs are all discussed by Perdonnet and Polonceau in their second edition of 1866. They warn against placing them at the end of the platforms where they will not be noticed and recommend they should be clearly visible, though 'surrounded, if one wishes, as in Germany, by a little garden'.

The type of passenger varied from station to station, and season to season. Sir John Betjeman in *First and Last Loves* says of Paddington: 'Its passengers are nearly all country people', while at St Pancras 'guncases and fishing rods go north with tweed-clad lairds, salmon and game returning in the guard's van without them'. John Pendleton describes York 'in summer and autumn' as 'the halting-place of a multitude, full of the anticipation of enjoyment, on their way to the seaside . . . Later it is thronged with hunting men and there is the rattle of horse-boxes in the sidings. At Convocation the platform is crowded with bishops and clergy.'

York is also of interest for its unusual layout, built on a curve, according to Sampson's *Guide to York* of 1893, to allow trains to pass through without the 'backing, changing and causing inconvenience which had to be endured at the old station'. As a result of the length and curve of the platforms it was 'impossible to see trains approach either end of the station with certainty' and they had to be worked out by signals. A signal-box was placed on the centre of the entrance platform combined with a bookstall; on the north side was another signal-box with a flower and fruit stall below. The ends of York's curving train sheds, like most of the great British and Continental train sheds illustrated in this volume, were glazed across to prevent the 'effects of violent winds' (the principal exception is Milan).

At York, as elsewhere, the four different roofs, all semicircular and of varying width, denoted the different types of traffic. The largest, according to Sampson, covered the north and south through traffic; the northern span covered three lines for local through trains; while the two southern spans were of three lines and two lines respectively.

Before the advent of the trolley, porters played a crucial part in the life of every major railway station and guidebooks are full of hints as to whether, or what, they should be tipped. Ivatts, in his *Railway Management*, lamented how 'a poor woman, a third-class passenger with a baby on her left arm and one or two baskets and bundles on the other arm, may groan under her load along the platform, while a young, foppish, muscular Christian, alighting from a first-class carriage cannot be allowed by the porters to carry his light dressing bag across the platform to a cab.' His proposed solution (as already happened in some places) was to give certain porters special uniforms marked 'porter for third-class passengers'. As well as station porters there was also a category of outside or badge porters 'of great service to passengers who have only a short distance to go outside the station and whose means prevent them hiring a cab or omnibus'.

The arrangements for baggage varied from one country to another. Murray's *Handbook to Northern Germany* in 1877 complains: 'Many of the German rules and regulations are in the highest degree cumbrous, frivolous and vexatious, none more so than those relating to overweight of baggage . . . Travellers should be at the station, if they have luggage, some time before the train starts, as the weighing, ticketing and paying for the luggage is a very tedious process.' By contrast Murray's 1877 *Handbook* strongly approves the arrangements for arriving passengers at the Hamburger Bahnhof in Berlin. Cars and omnibuses were in waiting and 'a metal ticket is handed to the traveller corresponding to the number of the cab he is entitled to in his turn'.

Everybody's Paris, published in 1902, notes that first class passengers will rarely have difficulty in securing a porter 'but at busy seasons second and third class passengers may find themselves neglected'. Parisian porters, the guide continues, 'are easily distinguished by their uniforms, grey or blue, according to the company to which they belong,

peaked caps, and leather belts, either around their waists, or across their shoulders . . . They are required to behave civilly to travellers, and to give them any information they very reasonably expect.'

All the platforms, passages and approaches to a station had to be swept once a day, and at some large stations, Ivatts says, badge porters were required to do this in return for the grant of access to the station. The night and early morning, when few passengers were about, were considered the best time for sweeping, so the duty also fell on night porters. Windows also had to be cleaned at fixed times, and all paint-work had to be regularly scoured either by porters or painters. 'Dirty dusty platforms spoil passengers' clothes, dirty windows and dirty paint offend the eye, and give a station and those who manage it a bad name.' Ivatts recommended 'two or three navy pensioners as porters, who, having been accustomed to wash ships' decks, take cheerily to such kind of work.'

Inside cleaning was usually deputed to women, perhaps porters' wives or widows. Looking-glasses were to be dusted in the corners, grates cleaned and black-leaded, lamp globes washed, walls and cornices brushed down. Lamp rooms required a special effort to keep them clean. Ivatts recommended tiled or concrete floors but if tiles were too cold for the men's feet 'small wooden gratings, like those used on board steamships, might be supplied'. All this I quote to show the effort devoted to ensuring that stations were attractive places. 'A station should have a clean, bright, cheerful appearance', Ivatts said. Shrubs in boxes helped decorate a station and where a railway company had waste land a working nursery gardener could at a very small outlay produce plenty of shrubs at a small yearly cost. Old photographs of stations, taken at the turn of the century, show them filled with shrubs in window-boxes and baskets of flowers. 'At terminal stations', Ivatts concluded in a flight of imagination, 'fountains would prove an adornment and in summer contribute to cool the atmosphere.'

Many Victorian train-sheds are now black with age and grime. The ironwork has not been repainted for years, the glass has been replaced either by corrugated plastic, or wire-strengthened glass, both of which reduce the amount of light. But in the 19th century stations were bright and colourful. John Pendleton says of St Pancras in *Our Railways* (1894): 'The roof has no less than two and a half acres of glass in it. The ironwork and woodwork are painted in pretty sky-tints. The great span is light in colour and graceful in form.' At York, while the city was 'grey with antiquity', the station was 'attractive from its brightness, its light lines and the harmoniousness of its colouring'. York, Pendleton concluded, was a 'gentleman among stations'. Today, the brightly painted capitals of the cast-iron columns of York give a sense of the colourful-

King's Cross in 1860: noise, bustle and excitement – the Railway Age at its peak.

ness of Victorian stations, as does the train-shed at Brighton with its dramatic red roof.

Stations could also be bright at night. Today Manchester Central is decaying and forlorn (though soon to take on a new life as a conference hall) but in 1894 Pendleton wrote: 'At night when the station approaches are illuminated with arc lights, and the ticket "sheds", refreshment rooms and bookstalls with incandescent lamps, it looks almost brilliant.' Baedeker's *London and its Environs* in 1889 observed that most of London's fourteen principal railway stations 'are now lighted by electric light'.

Cheerful staff, responsive to passengers' enquiries, were no less important than bright paint and good lighting. Ivatts recommended 'one or two policemen, able and willing to answer questions, posted at suitable places between the booking office and the departure platforms. Men of a talkative turn of character are the most efficient, and Irishmen fill this kind of post well.' Cyril Bruyn Andrews in *The Railway Age* (1937) recalls policemen 'in green uniforms' on duty at Brighton Station, giving directions to passengers. This use of policemen in public buildings and places was common at the time: a photograph of about 1902 illustrated in Marjorie Caygill's *The Story of the British Museum*, 1981, shows museum security staff mixed with officers seconded from Metropolitan Police D Division.

According to *Everybody's Paris* (1902), each large station in the capital was provided with several interpreters. 'They are to be recognized by their uniform, much like that of a hotel-porter and their caps with the word *Interprète* in gold letters.' Murray's 1876 *Handbook* to Holland cautions strangers to 'be on their guard against the voluntary guides and hotel touts who infest railway stations, steamboat wharves, etc. They are for the most part consummate blackguards.'

In France Mark Twain was profoundly impressed by the orderliness at stations. 'Every third man wears a uniform, and whether he be a Marshal of the Empire or a brakeman he is perfectly willing to answer all your questions with tireless politeness.'

Arrivals were most complicated at large international stations, if the visitor had to take luggage through the customs. 'Take the cab or omnibus, on the left of the arrival platform,' counsels *Everybody's Paris*, 'and leave one of the party on guard, for thieves are constantly waiting to snatch dressing cases, hand-bags, etc, and go to the customs house.' Most English visitors were likely to bring a small quantity of tea with them, and were advised to have it in their handluggage and make a speedy exit through the *rien a déclarer* exit. As France was a protectionist country they were advised to wear new shoes an hour before packing and warned that matches were a Government monopoly in France and importing them strictly forbidden.

Ivatts had often seen 'at large English stations, porters who seem perfectly weary and worn out with answering questions . . . these kind of men are out of place on a passenger platform, and should be sent to a goods shed to load goods'. Goods work was in fact as important a part of the life of the great termini as passengers – though as freight switched to road this tended to be forgotten. Often in evidence was a huge milk traffic. 'Certain platforms at Waterloo used to smell of sour milk for most of the day', Philip Unwin observes in *Travelling by Train in the Edwardian Age* (1979). Several of the London termini had huge goods stations immediately adjoining. At King's Cross *The Great Northern Railway Guide* (1912) describes 'extensive granaries and a vast range of wharfage along the Regent's Canal; also the largest wholesale potato market to be found in London.' *The Great Eastern Railway Guide* of 1892 boasts of the huge goods terminus at Bishopsgate, next to Liverpool Street Station with one of the largest warehouses in London and 'almost equally capacious premises at Spitalfields'. St Pancras was raised up on arches to take trains over the Regent Canal and under these according to Murray's *Handbook to London* of 1874 ran 'two stories of warehouses for Bass & Co.'s Burton Pale Ale'.

The marvel of the great termini and stations illustrated in this book is that, with the single exception of Manchester Central, they are still in use. The stations of America's leading cities were no less awe inspiring, and sometimes on an even more colossal scale, but with the glorious exception of New York's Grand Central virtually all of them have closed or all but closed for railway use. Many have taken on a new vigorous lease of life through conversion to alternative use, and may be better cared for and in better condition than for many years. But Europe's great termini and stations still are the busiest points of a still popular transport system. Not all have kept their character in equal degree, and even when the building is well maintained small thoughtless alterations can cumulatively do terrible damage and indeed demean them to such an extent that few people pause to enjoy them as buildings. Manfred Hamm's photographs, however, show just how much there is still to appreciate if one takes the time to look, whether in grand perspectives or small details. The message of these photographs is that with sensitive treatment these buildings can retain their original grandeur yet function in a modern age. Looking at just one or two stations it is not easy to understand just how spectacular and how subtle was the achievement of their designers and builders. Compared one against the other the full inventiveness and range becomes apparent. For nearly a century Europe's historic stations have almost been ignored except in specialized works. The photographs in this book prompt us to put this to rights.

BRITAIN

Iron roofs are the glory of the great British stations. Whatever changes for good or ill take place below, they survive with their drama and beauty unimpared. Brighton, with its vivid red ironwork, is the most eyecatching of them all (15, 16) and is all the more sensational for being on a curve. The girders of the roof spring from slender columns, so that a spectator standing at the end sees the arches springing from the columns one after another in dazzlingly quick succession. This perspective gives the impression that the columns themselves are linked by further arches, like the aisle of a medieval church, but this is not the case: the girders spanning the distance between columns and helping to bear the weight of the roof are flat, though they are supported by curved angle brackets.

York takes the drama of Brighton a stage further (17-20). The curve of the platforms is even more pronounced and continuous, so the train-shed disappears out of sight. The spans between the columns are more elaborately treated: instead of simple cross-braced girders there is tracery picked out in white. The girders of the roof are pierced with quatrefoils, circles and stars to increase the decorative effect. But the climax of the ornament comes in the flowing acanthus brackets emblazoned with the initials of the North Eastern Railway.

While Brighton and York still pulsate with trains Manchester Central (21, 22, 23) has stood empty and derelict for years. Now there are exciting plans for its restoration as a major conference centre but even in its agony of debris and broken glass it retains a silent majesty. What is remarkable in terms of construction is the way the great girders of the roof slice through the side walls of the station, letting light through on either side. And though the platform canopies beyond the train-shed have all but disappeared the columns and brackets have survived.

Bristol Temple Meads, also on a curve (24), has a similar drama. Here the arched roof is broad and low with turrets and crenellations adding an exotic note, and the pinnacles of the tower visible over the roofs.

In Glasgow (25-28) the sturdy riveted columns no longer try to look like the stone columns of ancient temples – though they still have correct classical capitals. Above, the ironwork is more forceful with great semi-circular lunettes spanning each pair of bays.

Taller, lighter and airier than Brighton or York are the great sheds at Paddington (29). As at York, drama comes from the sheer number of train-sheds ranged side by side but the brilliance of Paddington is the way the cross vistas are opened up – like the transepts of a cathedral – so there are views across the station as well as along. But nowhere is the cathedral analogy so apt as at Liverpool Street Station (30, 31). Here the slender pairs of columns set on pedestals taller than a man, carry the great spans of the train-sheds as well as lesser girders linking each pair of columns and filled with delicate pierced tracery. These cross views are continued by the transverse roofs over the platforms at the side of the station and the effect is completed by the trio of arched windows in the flanking wall.

At Paddington and Liverpool Street the sense of lightness is increased by the sheer expanse of glass. Completely in contrast is St Pancras, the most forceful and overpowering of all the British train-sheds – a Durham compared to a Gloucester or a Salisbury. St Pancras steals the breath by its sheer span. It is too broad and massive to spring from slender columns (32, 33). Heavy brick supports are built out to carry the weight of the descending girders. The side walls are impenetrably solid, though given polychrome richness by the red and white of the almost Moorish arches. The experience of St Pancras is completed by the extraordinary structures which stand at either end of it. Just beyond the station mouth to the north is a wonderful trio of early gas cylinders, three great circles of Doric columns linked by trellis-pattern cross-girders, rising in three elegant tiers. Gas cylinders are almost everyone's idea of a blot on the landscape but these, painted in brilliant black, red and white, have the plumage of an Ivanhoe. And it is precisely the world of medieval chivalry and romance that the great station hotel at the south end of St Pancras evokes. Here stepped gables, turrets, spires, dormers, finials and clusters of chimneys combine to create a silhouette as magical as the Houses of Parliament or the Law Courts in the Strand. But sheer brilliance of colour – rose pink brick, flashing white stone and crisp leadwork – makes St Pancras Europe's most dazzling railway station.

Previous page: London, King's Cross

22 · Manchester, Central Station

24 · Bristol, Temple Meads

GERMANY

'The German civic authorities, unlike those in Great Britain, assisted the railways to provide adequate main stations, which were regarded as the principal entrances to the cities, by donating land to provide impressive frontages with adequate open spaces.' So runs a revealing passage in the volume on *Ports and Communications* on Germany in the *Geographical Handbook* series published by the Naval Intelligence Division in May 1945. 'The central station at Frankfurt-am-Main', our unknown author continues, 'was the finest terminus in Europe at its opening in 1888, but the Leipzig station now takes pride of place, although it is rivalled by those of several other cities, such as Königsberg.'

Despite the devastation of allied bombing in the Second World War, some great termini survive in Germany as witnesses to the grandeur of the architecture of the *Reichsbahn*. Frankfurt is illustrated here with its wonderful parade of symmetrically arranged train-sheds – three wide spans in the centre and lesser ones at either end (49). In contrast to most English termini the glass screen at the mouths, sheltering station users from the bitter winter conditions of central Europe, comes down almost to the level of the trains. Inside, the great iron roofs rise not from columns as at Liverpool Street station, nor from buttresses as at St Pancras. Instead the arc of the girders continues in an unbroken sweep right down to the platforms – narrowing almost to a point, so that in a virtuoso engineering flourish the whole weight of the roof is seen to be carried on the smallest possible point. The idea of narrowing supports as they near the ground, reversing the traditional ideas of loadbearing, had found its finest expression in the great Machinery Hall of the Paris International Exhibition of 1889, now long vanished, and the roofs at Frankfurt stand as its memorial.

The same system is in evidence in the great sheds at Leipzig (1906-1915), though here the metal structure is still lighter and more skeletal, opening up majestic vistas through a seeming infinity of arches (42-43). Leipzig was once the busiest station in all Europe, but now with the division of Germany and Europe it is eerily silent and the platforms illustrated here are all but deserted. The former importance of Leipzig is apparent too in the huge concourse building, more than a thousand feet long. The great façade swelling out in a series of bows is at once Baroque in its movement, and Neoclassical in its severity. At either end the projecting wings with tall windows announcing lofty concourses within have the look of turbine halls – a hint of Peter Behrens's famous AEG Turbine Factory in Berlin, built in 1909.

At Bremen (54, 55), dexterity of a different kind comes into play – the problem of clothing the great arc of the train-shed with the vocabulary of a conventional architectural style. Turin and Seville (illustrated later) represent two brilliant solutions to this problem – but working in the iron and glass idiom of the station roof. At Bremen the architect has sought to superimpose the *Rundbogenstil*, the round-arched style popular in public buildings, and has done so with startling success. The play between larger and smaller arches – all semicircular – encompassed within the broader flattened arch of the train-shed is brilliant and the detail is as good as the overall design. Two tones of brickwork provide colourful contrast with the white stonework of the inner arcades and the great spandrels inset with carved figures. If only, one muses, the clock face could be more in keeping with the rest of the front, now so resplendently cleaned. Worth noting too is the brickwork of the arches, fanning out in a perfect arc, bearing comparison with Saarinen's memorable station front at Helsinki.

Previous page: Leipzig, Hauptbahnhof

40 · Leipzig, Hauptbahnhof

42 · Leipzig, Hauptbahnhof

44 · Leipzig, Hauptbahnhof

46 · Leipzig, Bayrischer Bahnhof

48 · Berlin, Hamburger Bahnhof

50 · Frankfurt-am-Main, Hauptbahnhof

Frankfurt-am-Main, Hauptbahnhof · 51

52 · Frankfurt-am-Main, Hauptbahnhof

54 · Bremen, Hauptbahnhof

56 · Cologne, Hauptbahnhof

58 · Hamburg, Dammtor Bahnhof

60 · Hamburg, Hauptbahnhof

FINLAND

Finnish Railway Stations are the subject of a charming monograph published by the National Board of Antiquities, *Suomen Rautatieasemat Vuosina 1857-1920*. Numerous original architects' drawings as well as photographs show delightful country stations, almost all of timber construction, with pretty fretwork on the canopies and porticoes and highly distinctive window heads and glazings. Any one, it seems, would serve immediately as the setting for a film of a great 19th-century Russian novel – for Finland at this time was a Russian Grand Duchy.

The main railway station at Helsinki is something quite different – the climax of the National Romantic Movement in Finnish architecture, the visible embodiment of a nation's yearnings for independence. The style is at once Nordic yet quite distinct from the rest of Scandinavian architecture – rather like the Finnish language. In its rugged romanticism it has an uncanny resemblance to the expressive masonry architecture of H.H. Richardson in America.

The competition for the station was won in 1904 by Gesellius, Lindgren and Saarinen, but in the event the station was built to revised designs by Saarinen alone in 1907-14. In 1908 Saarinen had visited both Josef Olbrich, who had by this time moved to Darmstadt from Vienna,

and Peter Behrens in Berlin – Helsinki station is not without overtones of *Jugendstil*.

The hallmark of the station front is its superb masonry. The architect has clearly decided and drawn out the exact size and shape of every stone. Around the great arched window over the main entrance the stonework opens out like a fan, each stone measured to be identical in width to its neighbour. Saarinen sought to increase the sense of mass by stepping the front both outwards and inwards, with concentric arches emphasizing the centrepiece and rich mouldings around the huge deep set windows.

With a classical building, cornices, balustrades and plinths all create a strong horizontal emphasis: here the lines are predominantly vertical. The wave pattern carved on the shafts encasing the giants is echoed on the wall behind them by notched bands running straight through the coping stones.

As befitted the age of electricity Helsinki station was designed to pronounce its role by night as well as by day. The giants hold globes that light up by night and the great central window unmistakably proclaims the station entrance.

Previous page: Helsinki, Rautatieasema Järnvägsstation

RAUTATIE

64 · Helsinki, Rautatieasema Järnvägsstation

66 · Helsinki, Rautatieasema Järnvägsstation

ITALY

'There are a good many things about this Italy I cannot understand', wrote Mark Twain in his *Pleasure Trip to the Continent* (1871), 'and more especially I cannot understand how a bankrupt government can have such palatial railroad depôts and such marvels of turnpikes. The depôts are vast palaces of cut marble, with stately colonnades of the same royal stone traversing them from end to end, and with walls and ceilings richly decorated with frescoes. The lofty gateways are graced with statues, and the broad floors are all laid in polished flags of marble.'

Genoa's Stazione Principe is just such a grand classical palace, and very much a response to the architectural traditions of the city it serves. One of the great features of 17th- and 18th-century palaces in Genoa was airy, spacious staircases, opening directly on to arcaded courtyards. The grand entrance illustrated here (69) provides just such an eyecatching perspective of a staircase glimpsed through a great archway and screen of columns beyond. Outside, the main elevation is soberly Doric and enrichment is concentrated in the attic storey (70) where four allegorical figures, carved with superb realism, support the pediment. The ornament of the archway and frieze above has great precision and delicacy, and the same crispness of detail is seen in the splendid griffins supporting the station clock and the acanthus swirls on either side. The station hall (72), with an arcade at first floor level, is suggestive of the *cortile* of a handsome town palace. The treatment of square piers and broad panelled pilasters rather than columns or half columns is distinctly North Italian.

At Turin, the great beauty lies in the architectural treatment of the curved end of the train-shed (75). It is particularly interesting to compare this with Bremen (54), where the train-shed is articulated by boldly modelled archways in strong red brickwork. Here the end wall is more like a lace veil drawn across the span, though the play of arches within arches is very similar. The structure is made as light as possible, with slender, almost Gothic, colonnettes rather than massive piers. The glazing of the windows also has a Gothic flavour with ogee arches at the bottom and interlacing pointed arches above. All this is seen to particularly good effect at night when the front is floodlit, yet with a faint warm glow of light showing through from behind.

The most ambitious of the Italian stations is undoubtedly Milan, completed only in 1931. Milan station, states the *Geographical Handbook* of the Naval Intelligence Division, 'is reputed to be the largest and most magnificent of all European stations. Each line has two platforms, one 24 feet wide exclusively reserved for passengers, the other 13 feet wide for luggage and ancillary services . . . the station has a palatial booking-hall, magnificent waiting rooms, restaurant, cafés, bars . . . '

Milan station is an archetypical example of a particular brand of architecture, popular early this century, which sought to achieve monumental effects through an emphasis on mass. Columns which might be free standing are embedded in the wall (81); attics which might have had open balustrades are completely solid (80). There is a tremendous play on cubes and rectangles: much of the architectural detail is deliberately blockish. Inside, this emphasis on solids creates a somewhat sepulchral mood, but is full of atmosphere none the less. The great staircase illustrated here (82-83) might be an architectural set dreamed up for a Hollywood epic of Ancient Rome or Egypt in the 1920s, the very years in which Milan station was rising. Twenty years ago such a comparison would only have been made in an unflattering sense – but today Milan station can be appreciated for what it is, railway architecture at its most imperial.

Previous page: Genoa, Stazione Piazza Principe

Genoa, Stazione Piazza Principe · 69

70 · Genoa, Stazione Piazza Principe

72 · Genoa, Stazione Piazza Principe

74 · Turin, Stazione Porta Nuova

76 · Milan, Stazione Centrale

78 · Milan, Stazione Centrale

84 · Milan, Stazione Centrale

SPAIN

Spain's comparative isolation from the rest of Europe has meant that again and again she has taken architectural styles – Gothic, Renaissance, Mannerist and Baroque – and put her own distinctive stamp on them, developing them quite separately from the mainstream. This is true of railway architecture. Spain's best railway stations are highly individual compositions and as these photographs show, survive, thanks to an innate conservatism, remarkably complete. Best of all, the Spanish sense of dignity has meant that they are hardly disfigured by signs, hoardings, placards and the general clutter that so mars stations in other European countries, especially Britain. The most remarkable is undoubtedly Toledo (93), with its great centrepiece of horseshoe arches stepped back layer by layer. The windows within have tracery of immense elaboration: outside, lanterns still hang from iron brackets. The centrepiece is of stone below and brick above – long narrow bricks like those the Romans used. But at the corners the surface is cut away to reveal patches of different kinds of masonry, some set in rough uneven courses, others in neat rectangular blocks. It is a technique reminiscent of one of Piranesi's engravings of Ancient Rome.

The Moorish detailing continues inside with the wonderful lattern screen fronting the ticket office (94). The tiled floor and tiled dado also remain intact, as do the ironwork grilles introduced to ensure that passengers made an orderly queue on one side and departed on the other.

Moorish Revival is equally in evidence in the handsome station in Seville (92). Here too are the horseshoe arches – though without the notches – and the zig-zag crenellations like little stylized Christmas trees. Seville is also an interesting and successful example of the architectural clothing of a train-shed, this time in Moorish Gothic, neatly sandwiched between the corner pavilions of the station front.

At Valencia the station interior is the Spanish equivalent of *Stile Liberty* or Jugendstil (91) – a little more rectilinear than French or Belgian Art Nouveau. The ticket office, visible at the back of the left-hand picture, is not without a touch of the great Glaswegian architect and designer Charles Rennie Mackintosh, whose work was so influential on the Continent. One of his particular mannerisms was to carry the vertical members upwards so they projected like finials, just as they do here. The lights around the column in the foreground are hung from brackets in the shape of the prow of a ship – this is a deliberate pun on the rostral columns of Ancient Rome which had ships' prows projecting in this way. Also very much *de l'époque* is the mosaic work with stylized Arts-and-Crafts flowers and parting message for foreign visitors.

The interior of Barcelona's Estacion del Norte (89) again has the blockish look of *Stile Liberty* with the vertical piers continued as up-turned brackets. Here the ticket kiosk is an almost free-standing structure, and the iron railings in front looking almost like prie-dieux suggest for a moment a series of confessionals.

Barcelona's Francia station (88) has a memorable train-shed which curves out of sight like York or Brighton station in England (15 and 19), though here the atmosphere is quite different as there is no daylight visible at the end and little natural light from above.

Previous page: Barcelona, Estaçion de Francia

88 · Barcelona, Estaçion de Francia

92 · Seville, Estaçion de Huelva

PORTUGAL

Railway stations rarely figure in guidebooks but any visitor to Lisbon walking down the city's Champs-Elysées, the Avernida da Liberdade, towards Rossio Square, the hub of the city centre, must stop for a moment and wonder at the astonishing front of the Rossio Station. Immediately opposite the National Theatre, it looks at first glance like a princely palace or great town hall (97), with its tall first floor windows and balconies seemingly designed for appearances before the crowd. But the two great intertwined horseshoe arches below, like the entrances to a railway tunnel, give away its true function and there, woven into the rich ornamental surrounds, are the words Estação Central. The style is Neo-Manueline, a revival of the exotic and highly individual brand of Gothic mingled with Renaissance which flourished in Portugal in the early 16th century. Here Gothic is dominant, with buttresses, pinnacles and pointed arches, as well as a gloriously rich pierced ornament along the parapet, but the first floor windows rest on classical columns and above are Renaissance-style portrait roundels.

Inside the great entrance doors, the station is wholly modern but on the first floor grand rooms survive adapted as a bar and restaurant and, seated in great leather armchairs, glass of port in hand, it is possible to savour a lingering sense of the comfort of rail travel in the age in which the station was built. The platforms are higher still, for Rossio station is built against one of Lisbon's numerous hills, and here is a handsome train-shed still full of atmosphere, where details such as the shields above the columns (95) survive unaltered.

Just as the Rossio station harks back to Lisbon's famous Hieronymite Monastery and the Tower of Belem on the Tagus, so the St Benedict Station at Oporto takes inspiration from the numerous Baroque churches in the city which are entirely clad in tiles portraying religious scenes. Like so much in Portugal the date is unexpectedly late and the fascinating *azulejos* in the station hall were painted in 1930. They portray great historical events such as King João I's entry into Oporto and the Portuguese capture of Ceuta, the stronghold of the barbary pirates, which assured them control of the straits of Gibraltar. Other panels portray scenes of everyday life – harvesting, fruitpicking and fishing – while opposite are a series of panels portraying engines billowing plumes of steam.

Previous page: Lisbon, Estacão do Rossio

98 · Porto, Estação de São Bento

100 · Porto, Estação de São Bento

FRANCE

The expression *limoger* came into currency in the First World War, meaning to supersede or send to a backwater – when unwanted generals were retired from the front to Limoges. The station at Limoges, (105) inaugurated in 1929, seems built to announce to the world that Limoges is no provincial cul-de-sac, but a flourishing centre to rival spas and resorts like Vichy and Cannes. In a fascinating issue of *Monuments Historique* (1978 No.6) devoted to stations it is described as a '*chef d'oeuvre neo-byzantine*'. Exotic it is, and it belongs with a whole series of public buildings of Beaux-Arts derivation in an exaggerated Louis-Seize Neoclassical. The Grand Palais and the Petit Palais beside the Seine with their stupendous roofs are two of the most familiar examples, but it was a style used widely for casinos and grand hotels. Recurring subjects in the great Beaux-Arts competitions were designs for monuments, towers and lighthouses and the great clock tower at Limoges is a reflection of this. But if Limoges Benedictins will always be too heavy or extravagant for some palates, what is undeniable is the excellent quality of the materials and the pristine condition in which they are kept.

Tours station (107) is a whited sepulchre of a different kind. Here, just as at King's Cross in London, the arcs of the train-sheds are made the predominant feature of the entrance front. But the problem of marrying them with classical forms is handled in an unusually bold and ingenious way. The train-sheds are framed by giant columns surmounted by statues, rather like the piers that are found on contemporary bridges. But though these columns, with their pedestals, rise well above the three storey buildings on either side they are none the less in their proportions, dwarf columns. Inside, Tours, like Limoges, is well maintained and a pleasure to the eye.

It is of course the great termini in Paris which take pride of place among French stations. The Gare du Nord built in 1861-65 is a characteristic example of the French genius for showing off public buildings to advantage. With its crisp, chaste detailing, it could be a museum or university (108). Only the great triangular silhouette of the centrepiece hints at something different, and once inside all is explained, for it takes its shape from the great barn-like train-shed (109). While most of the major European train-sheds have arched roofs, those of the Gare du Nord are flat and sloping, but the span is so large that two rows of slender columns have been introduced to support it. Yet, if the roof is much more commonplace than many of its peers it has, through sheer scale and openness, a tremendous power and drama. It brings to mind Inigo Jones's famous remark to the Duke of Bedford on being asked to design a church which was quite simple, not much more than a barn. 'If you will have a barn, Sir,' Inigo Jones replied, 'I will build you the greatest barn in Christendom.'

The Gare de l'Est, built in 1847-52 (114-115), was in its prime regarded as the finest station in the world. It is perhaps the most perfect of all marriages of a classical front with a boldly expressed train-shed, and the ironwork of the great window in the centre of the entrance front deserves comparison in its boldness with the rose windows of medieval cathedrals.

The Gare de Lyon, built in 1897-1900, stands for a later epoch (101) and its great campanile clocktower is a model for Limoges-Benedictins. The exterior is intended to impress rather than to charm but inside the attention given to detail is an endless source of fascination and delight. The ironwork is endlessly varied – on the open staircase leading up to the famous restaurant (110), in the columns and ribs supporting the roof, and the brackets carrying the station clocks (111). But the lightest touch of all is the elegant naked lady airing her flowing locks oblivious of the express train which is pounding up behind her.

Previous page: Paris, Gare de Lyon

Limoges, Gare de Limoges-Bénédictins · 103

104 · Limoges, Gare de Limoges-Bénédictins

110 · Paris, Gare de Lyon

Paris, Gare de Lyon · 111

112 · Paris, Gare de Lyon

BELGIUM

The architecture of Belgium is highly idiosyncratic: rarely in Brussels or Antwerp is there an even row of houses designed as a single composition. Instead each house is different from its neighbour, often violently so. And the Low Countries are the home of Mannerism, the style that replaced Renaissance simplicity and elegance with complexity, contradiction, extravagance and a liberal dose of the grotesque.

Antwerp station is designed with just such contrariness (122). No train-shed is visible from the street, but rising boldly from the roof is a powerful dome resting on great glazed lunettes, looking like the glass ends of train-sheds. Indeed the pattern of the glazing, a series of lozenges, narrow at one end and broad at the other, seems directly inspired by the great train-shed of the Gare de l'Est in Paris (114-115). Here in fact is a dome designed to proclaim the use of the building below, what the French call *architecture parlante*.

From the street the building is given added interest by the two octagonal turrets with stone-roofed domes, in character immediately recalling the memorable pink terracota domes on the turrets of Harrods store in London. A date plaque (119) proclaims the year 1905, and by this time this form of Mannerism was international. The Brompton Road front of Harrods dates from 1902; the rich detailing of the Antwerp station equally echoes the interior of Frank Matcham's Coliseum Theatre in London, dating from 1904. Every detail has to be activated and made busy: the arch has a whole series of keystones, any stretch of blank wall is filled with a plaque or tablet. Scrolls and brackets are everywhere. Gilded trophies abound.

By contrast the great train-shed is simple and severe. The iron ribs detach from the walls and form a great arc over the platforms. But the walls behind rise sheer and are filled with huge glass windows. All this is in complete contrast to the earlier great English train-sheds where walls are solid and windows, if any, relatively small. But the progression is fascinating in itself and parallels in its own way the development of Europe's cathedrals from Romanesque to Gothic and the steady reduction of the wall to allow ever increasing areas of glass.

Previous page: Antwerp, Centraal Station

120 · Antwerp, Centraal Station

122 · Antwerp, Centraal Station

HOLLAND

After the massive iron and steel girders of great train-sheds all over Europe, Haarlem station is something quite different. Here is a soaring metal roof so light that it looks like a mesh of scaffolding – almost a temporary structure (129) rather than a major city station built to impress and endure. Usually the train-shed rises from the walls of the buildings on the platform's edge but here the roofs continue over them, high above. The station offices, waiting rooms and buffets are like free-standing pavilions huddling amidst the steel piers. But in design they are all the more charming for this, a mixture of stone, white and blue glazed brick, and elaborate woodwork. And the delight of the station is that the detail survives unaltered and well maintained (130). Brightly coloured tiled panels announce the waiting rooms of the different classes, the carved stonework of the archways survives in pristine condition. The wooden windows retain their small panes. The walls are not disfigured with advertisement placards – these are hung at right angles like inn signs (129). Even the signal box remains unaltered, perched high above the tracks.

At Amsterdam a virtue is made of advertisements in a different and altogether bolder way (126 and 127). Here the glazed ends of the train-shed are filled with giant red letters transparent enough to catch the light from behind, recalling the extraordinary bon-bon which hangs suspended over the platforms at Frankfurt (50). But the real excitement of Amsterdam is the Royal Entrance (125) still laid with richly piled carpet. Here is Gothic to rival the Midland hotel at St Pancras – marble balustrades and columns, brightly coloured stencilled vaults, painted scenes, rich plasterwork, finely carved woodwork and virtuoso ironwork.

Previous page: Haarlem

Historical and technical notes
on the stations illustrated

Axel Foehl

13 *London, King's Cross*

Great Britain was the nation in which the wheels of the Industrial Revolution began to turn. At the end of the eighteenth century it was the wheels of textile machinery and, from 1825 onwards, for the first time anywhere in the world, the wheels of steam-driven railways designed for the regular transport of passengers and goods. Engineers and architects were thus presented with the task of developing and designing not only new equipment and new machines but also new types of buildings. It was station buildings above all which provoked a lively discussion as to the relative priorities of architectural design for the frontage block on the one hand and constructional engineering for the train-shed on the other. One of the best examples of a style of architecture which is clearly functional in appearance is King's Cross Station, north-west of the City, designed by Lewis Cubitt in 1852 for the Great Northern Railway. The two huge semi-circular windows in the façade clearly reflect the profile of the two train-sheds behind them, and thus announce the *raison d'être* of a building which could not be anything other than a railway station. There is no more concise description of the building than that offered by Cubitt himself: 'Fitness for its purpose and the characteristic expression of that purpose'.

The clock tower between the arches in the centre of the façade indicates the new role which time now played in the industrial age: the mechanical punctuality of the timetable demanded precise timekeeping. The clock itself, which had been seen at the Great Exhibition of 1851, is said never to have told the same time as the clock at St Pancras, next door. When it was opened, King's Cross was the largest station in England and by around 1900 some 250 trains were using the station every day, most of them local or regional services. The situation was complicated by the narrow approach tunnel, the so-called Gas Works Tunnel, which passes under the Regent's Canal and which used to be responsible for constant delays. A second, inclined and sharply curved tunnel known as the 'Hotel Curve' was opened in 1878. A GNR employee was permanently engaged in the tunnel strewing sand on the rails as each train passed, so that the wheels of the following train would have sufficient grip. It was a particularly detested job in the age of steam.

15, 16 *Brighton*

One of the earliest examples of a typical terminus is the one designed by David Mocatta in 1840/1841 for Brighton, the southern terminus of the London & Brighton Railway. Two lines started out from here, providing a link between the metropolis and the south-coast town, which had been a popular resort well before the advent of the railways. The present train-shed was designed by H.E. Wallis in 1883 and erected on arched ribs over the original shed of 1841, which was removed only when the new structure had been completed. The same process was used much later in mining headframes. The two lines curve out from the terminus in different directions, an arrangement mirrored in the dynamic curves of the two train-sheds (15). The arched roof supports are painted red and rest on narrow iron columns. They appear to an observer to telescope together in a dramatic row in which the cast-iron supports themselves seem to be joined together longitudinally by arches (16). The grandiose iron architecture of Brighton Station reflects the popularity which this most important of English resorts has enjoyed over the years.

17, 18/19, 20 *York*

The idea of a curved ground plan for the train-shed reappears in the four bays of York Station, the widest of which is 24 metres and the tallest 15 metres high. At Newcastle, Thomas Prosser, who from 1857 to 1874 was chief architect of the North Eastern Railway, completed the work of the original architect John Dobson; he had been the first to use malleable rolled iron ribs. Prosser incorporated this idea in the structure which William Peachey completed at York in 1877. Every third rib rests on a sturdy iron column with a Corinthian capital (17); the intermediate ribs are joined by cross-girders. All the ribs are perforated by quatrefoil openings, which make them seem lighter in weight than they actually are and increase the amount of light which enters the building. Some of the brackets are decorated with the NER monogram (18/19). The nine-bay *porte cochère*, on the other hand, is an unimpressive affair, overshadowed by the neighbouring Royal Station Hotel (20). The formal imbalance between train-shed and frontage block could almost be regarded as a trademark of NER, although the impression of space inside the building surpasses even that of Brighton Station and entitles us to count York Station among the most splendid examples of Victorian station architecture. The train-shed at York is in an excellent state of repair and forms a worthy counterpart to the attractions on offer at the town's National Railway Museum, the largest railway museum in Europe. Housed in two of the finest surviving roundhouse locomotive sheds, the museum is run as a branch of the Science Museum in London.

21   Manchester, Victoria

Among the most confused and confusing of stations is Victoria Station in the centre of Manchester. Until the closure of the adjacent Exchange Station, Manchester Victoria Station was able to boast the longest platform in the British Isles. Entering the station at street level, the prospective traveller ascends to the raised platforms whose entire width is spanned by a single flat roof. This roof, which was partially removed in the 1930s and which suffered further damage during the Second World War, consists of horizontal cross girders perforated by floral patterns and supported on cast-iron pillars. Over the girders lie curved ribs upon which the flat ridge-and-furrow roof rests. Illustration 21 shows the structure quite clearly, together with a narrow platform building with clocks. This building used also to be under the main roof prior to its partial demolition, signs of which are still visible in the photograph. The train-shed was built in 1881 for the Lancashire & Yorkshire Railway. The four-storey frontage block was added by William Dawes in 1909, its valancing still bearing the names of the former destinations of the Lancashire & Yorkshire Railway: Hull, Belgium and Liverpool appear here side by side in Art Nouveau lettering.

22, 23   Manchester, Central Station

In 1880 three railway companies, the Midland, the Manchester Sheffield & Lincolnshire, and the Great Northern, combined to form the Cheshire Lines Committee and build Manchester Central Station. Since the latter was the northern end of the stretch of track running from St Pancras in the south (32–36), its design was modelled on that of the London terminus. Like St Pancras, Manchester too got a single span train-shed, spanning (in this case) nine platforms and fifteen rails. It was 168 metres long, and its 64-metre span and 30-metre maximum height made it the second largest train-shed in England. Probably designed by Sir John Fowler, who was later one of the engineers of the Forth Bridge (1882–1889), the train-shed at Manchester Central Station is notable for the same peculiarities in its construction as those of its counterpart in London. The sturdy roof-ribs are tied by the platform floor, which is effectively at first-floor level, and form a huge framework which acts against

the horizontal thrust of the roof. Like York, Manchester Central lacks an impressive frontage: wooden buildings, originally intended as a temporary measure, continued to serve their purpose for decades. A hotel which had been planned for the site was eventually built opposite the station. The grandiose hall, with its ribs cut into the side walls, continued in use until 1969, when it was relegated to the status of a car-park. In 1982, however, a large-scale development was undertaken, involving a conference and exhibition centre intended to bring new life to the train-shed. Manchester's third largest station, Liverpool Road Station, built in 1830 and the oldest surviving station in the world, has also found a new use since 1983, when it became the home of the Greater Manchester Museum of Science and Industry.

24   Bristol, Temple Meads

One of the world's best-preserved examples of early station architecture is Temple Meads Station in Bristol. The engineer of the Great Western Railway, Isambard Kingdom Brunel (1806–1859), perhaps the leading engineer of the Victorian Age, was responsible for the seven-foot gauge of the track linking London and Bristol and designed all the buildings which bordered it. Temple Meads Station in Bristol is an early example of neo-Gothic architecture in a commercial building. Not only did Brunel design the frontage block in Tudor Gothic with its turrets and towers intended to harmonize with the city's historic buildings, he was further inspired by medieval architecture in his designs for the three-span train-shed whose iron supports and wooden roof are modelled on the 14th-century hammer-beam roof of London's Westminster Hall. Its span of 22 metres is two feet greater than that at Westminster. As a result, Temple Meads was regarded in its day as one of the best designed and best built stations of the time. The train-shed was used as a car-park during the 1960s and 1970s, but has now been turned into a national centre for engineering design by the Brunel Engineering Centre Trust with financial help from the city of Bristol and from British Rail. Brunel's basic design influenced all later developments to the station complex. The vast new iron train-shed was designed by Matthew Digby Wyatt and built between 1865 and 1878. Not only do the side walls of the newer shed take up Brunel's Gothic motifs, so, too, does the concourse building, not completed until 1935. Its pinnacles dwarf the shed behind it, presenting the observer with a fine example of the Tudor style. The awning over the platforms in the foreground dates from the final period of expansion between 1932 and 1935, and shows a standard form typical of the Great Western.

25, 26, 27, 28   Glasgow, Central Station

Glasgow Central was the headquarters of the Caledonian Railway (founded in 1845), which, together with the North British Railway, controlled the whole of the Scottish rail network. The Caledonian served the industrial conurbations of the Lowlands with their collieries, steel works and shipyards. Glasgow Central remains one of the busiest stations in Great Britain, and Glaswegians continue as before to meet on the station concourse by a First World War collecting box known as 'The Shell'. The train-shed by R. Rowand Anderson, completed in 1879, was later enlarged to accommodate thirteen platforms. Its steel trussed roof (27) was one of the first examples of a new type of construction which gradually replaced the earlier high-vaulted arched halls. Deep horizontal trusses supporting ridge-and-furrow glazing over the concourse and platforms avoid the need for supporting columns and thus ease the flow of passengers between the two areas. The train-shed was extended in 1899–1905 by James Miller: the new roof uses light-section trusses with elliptically curved ribs for longitudinal ridge-and-furrow glazing. Tall round-headed windows have been let into the side wall of the new shed which faces on to Hope Street (28). The five-storey Central Hotel rises up above the booking hall: it was built in 1883 and extended in 1907. Originally intended as offices, it soon became a part of what in Great Britain is the typically close architectural combination of station and hotel.

29 London, Paddington

Paddington is the second oldest of the major London stations, postdating King's Cross by only two years (13). We have already met its two designers: as in Bristol (24, 25), the engineer was Brunel and the architect Matthew Digby Wyatt. Stations were frequently described as 'cathedrals of technology', and the extent to which this description was justified will be clear to anyone who sees the 213-metre long train-shed at Paddington. Brunel designed a light and spacious three-bay shed, with two transepts framing the whole structure. A year after the completion of Paxton's Crystal Palace for the Great Exhibition of 1851, Brunel resolved to build what he himself called 'a large glasshouse adapted to suit the needs of the railways'. This shed followed the pattern set by Dobson's designs for Newcastle Station and later taken up by Prosser in York (17): every third rib rests on a column while the two intervening ribs are joined by cross-girders which are diagonally braced. The ribs are lavishly decorated on their lower sections with Wyatt's designs and at the height of the glass roof are pierced with openwork motifs. The capitals of the columns (restored in 1922) have a Moorish look to them. The two transepts each have a span of fifteen metres and serve as longitudinal supports. They were originally intended to take a set of large traversers for transferring rolling stock from one line to another, but were never used. Until 1920 the station

also boasted hydraulically operated bridges, designed by Brunel and used for passenger traffic between the platforms; they could be lowered each time a train passed. On the axis of the transepts were the directors' offices: oriel windows afforded them a view of the platforms. A fourth bay was added to the north of the existing train-shed in 1916, with a span of twelve metres, covering the taxi-cab approach road in London Street.

When Queen Victoria made her first railway journey in 1842, her destination was Paddington Station, albeit a forerunner of the present building, a wooden structure of modest dimensions which had been erected in 1838. At that time the Great Western Railway ran past Windsor on its way to Maidenhead, a distance of some twenty-two miles. The present station, completed in 1854, providing a fitting monument to the completed section of track which now ran as far as Bristol. It was also a memorial to the broad gauge of Isambard Kingdom Brunel, signs of which are still to be seen in the vast train-shed at Paddington. The strikingly large lamp holders there recall the pioneering role played by the Great Western in the introduction of electric lighting. As early as 1880, thirty-four electric lamps were being used to light the vast reaches of the Paddington train-shed, 213 metres long and 73 metres wide.

30/31 London, Liverpool Street

Liverpool Street Station affords examples of much that was technologically and architecturally significant in nineteenth-century station architecture, but it also offers the best opportunity to discuss the group of people for whom all these vast complexes are actually intended – the rail passengers themselves. Liverpool Street Station in the eastern part of the city and in the vicinity of what were once London's vast docklands was, and still is, the city's busiest passenger terminal. According to figures for 1975, more than 150,000 commuters use the station every day. In the heyday of rail travel in the 1920s there were a quarter of a million passengers every day, an inconceivable figure in our present age, blessed as it is with all the problems of individual travel. It may be said without exaggeration that Liverpool Street Station and the transport policies of the Great Eastern Railway are not only a piece of social history but an important factor in London's urban development. The history of whole areas of the city such as Leyton, Walthamstow and Ilford, formerly separate suburbs to the east of the metropolis, is closely bound up with the history of this one station. If the growth of these areas, with their hundreds of thousands of inhabitants, was primarily dependent upon the investment activities of private landowners and industrialists, one of the first prerequisites for such a development was the system of cheap transport which the railways provided for suburban commuters to get from their homes in the East End of London to their places of work in the centre of the city. Between 1881 and 1891 the population of Leyton rose by 113%, while the population of East Ham grew by 193% between 1891 and 1901. This growth was clearly related to the – frequently involuntary – low-price policies of the Great Eastern, and to the workmen's trains which arrived at Liverpool Street Station every morning and returned to the eastern suburbs every evening. The Parliamentary Act of 1864 which gave permission for the station to be built had made it a condition that the railway company should introduce cheap workmen's trains, initially as a compensation to the 5,000 or so Londoners who were made homeless by the building programme and who were now to be allowed to commute cheaply from their new homes in the suburbs to their old places of work in the city. These trains were so heavily used that the company was forced to lay on as many as 104 trains a day. This had certainly not been the company's initial intention, since they had hoped for higher profits from passengers paying the full fare. The question of cheap trains soon became a matter for public debate: attempts on the part of the Great Eastern to keep their 'service' within strictly limited bounds had led to their restricting workmen's trains to the period between 5 and 7 o'clock in the morning. As a result, workers who took advantage of the cheap rate arrived in town far too early, and were then at a loss to know what to do before beginning work. The London County Council took up their cause, arguing for an extension to the cheap-rate period and describing the Great Eastern as 'the workman's London railway', while continuing to accuse the company of pandering to 'silk-hatted customers'. The focus of all these activities, Liverpool Street Station, had been built between 1873 and 1875 by Edward Wilson: its four pitched iron spans were the work of the famous Manchester firm of William Fairbairn. Like Paddington (28), the western bay at Liverpool Street had a transept (30, 31); but what is unique about Liverpool Street are the hollow iron columns arranged in pairs and used as fall-pipes to remove excess rainwater. Also unique is the roof, constructed of triangular girders, an idea which was borrowed from bridge building. The ribs rest on mushroom-like, richly ornamented brackets above the columns. The picture of a bright and empty train-shed is typical of Liverpool Street as it appears today: individual travel and the abandonment of steam locomotives with their smoke- and soot-laden atmosphere have driven away all memories of dark and dirty sheds packed with rush-hour commuters, a scene which was once typical of Liverpool Street Station.

32/33, 34, 35, 36   *London, St Pancras*

The last of London's main-line stations to be considered here is situated close to the first: Kings Cross and St Pancras are immediate neighbours

in Euston Road. Together with the huge gas containers of the Somers Bridge Gasworks, recently restored down to the very last detail, and the Regent's Canal to the north, St Pancras Station forms the third element of a vast museum of architecture chronicling the history of public services and transportation in London. So many superlatives have been lavished upon St Pancras that it is difficult to list even its most important aspects. The train-shed is 200 metres long, 73 metres wide and 70 metres to the point of the arch: it was the largest iron-built structure in the world until the 1889 Paris Exhibition, when it was surpassed by the Galerie des Machines. The adjoining hotel was the biggest neo-Gothic secular building in the British Isles, and the whole station was the first in the world to have an entire book written about it in 1968. St Pancras, which was opened in 1868, was the Midland Railway's gateway to London. Until then the company had not had its own station in the metropolis and had to rely upon expensive help from other railways. It was intended that this newly acquired independence should be put to the test in architectural matters, too. The train-shed (1866–1868) was the work of two engineers, William H. Barlow and R. M. Ordish: its roof ribs are secured invisibly by horizontal tie members beneath the platform floor, which is at first-floor level. The floor of the train-shed is constructed of iron plates and is in turn supported by 688 iron columns on brick piers. Until 1960 the ground floor was used as a store for Burton's beer, the size of a beer barrel having been the unit that determined the space between the columns. Not only the train-shed but the frontage of the building, too, was to outdo all competition. The Midland Grand Hotel was designed by George Gilbert Scott. The result was a 400-bed palace with vast reception halls, a frontage of Gothic windows (36) and an almost bizarre array of spires and pinnacles along the length of its roof (34). The huge building was completed in 1876. It had the most modern fittings of any hotel of the period: gas chandeliers, electric bells, rubbish chutes and hydraulically operated lifts all helped to create an atmosphere of luxury. No expense was spared in finding a manager from among the best that Europe could offer – a Herr Etzensberger from Venice, who had previously looked after steamboat passengers on the Nile. Although the Midland Grand Hotel had a smoking room for women as early as 1890, and the first revolving doors in London, it fell increasingly behind the times, and in 1935 was turned into offices. Only the main staircase now remains to tell of former glories. One other fact which has taken its place in the architectural history of St Pancras is evidence of what, by modern standards, might almost be seen as an act of irresponsibility. Several thousand private dwellings in Agar and Somers Town were pulled down to make room for the station, causing some 10,000 persons to be made homeless without any offer of compensation, thus adding to the overcrowding which was already a problem in the surrounding area. The episode attests to the inconsiderateness with which economic and technological 'progress' was undertaken in the nineteenth century. None of this is visible today. What remains is the overwhelming impression of a vast train-shed unencumbered by any additional fittings, and of a vast frontage block which, right down to the bricks, slates, ashlars and iron from which it was built, represented a unique advertisement for the Midland Railway and for the transport of goods which the company brought to the capital.

37, 39, 40/41, 42/43, 44, 45   *Leipzig, Hauptbahnhof*

There is no necessary contradiction in the idea of leaving Great Britain via St Pancras and setting foot on European soil in Leipzig's Hauptbahnhof, for Leipzig too can lay claim to superlatives. At the time of its completion in 1915 it was the largest station in Europe and probably the most expensive in the world. A king and a kaiser had formed an agreement in 1898: Prussia and Saxony would together build the new station, the city of Leipzig helping its monarch with a third of the Saxon share in the building costs. In the event the whole building cost 140 million marks; and Leipzig, an industrial centre noted for its trade fairs, finally saw an end to all the transport problems which had beset its inner city. Hitherto, six stations owned by different companies and situated at an average distance of two kilometres from each other had made life a misery for Leipzig's commuters. The building programme took nine years to complete and it was not until the middle of the First World War, on 4 December 1915, that the copestone was added to the eastern train-shed of the new station – the very stone which had served as the foundation stone of Dresden's old station of 1864, long since demolished. The building being jointly owned, the eastern train-shed was reserved for Saxony, with the western, or so-called Prussian, train-shed forming a symmetrical counterpart. This architectural division had been a precondition of the competition when it was announced in 1906; a further clause stipulated that the building 'should, as an imposing architectural monument to Leipzig's commercial status, bear witness to Germany's economic expansion'. The designs submitted by the two Dresden architects William Lossow and Max Hans Kühne, whose watchword was 'Light and Air', were accepted, with minor modifications, as the best solution to the problem, and it was agreed to start work on the project. The foundation stone was laid in 1909.

In order to provide adequate foundations for the reinforced concrete structure, 3,125 reinforced concrete piles were driven into the fine subsoil. Above them rose up the 300-metre-wide frontage block with separate vestibules for Saxony and Prussia. Flights of steps ten metres wide led from there to a raised cross-platform 275 metres long and 25 metres wide. To this transept were attached six parallel train-sheds, each of them over 40 metres wide (42/43) and separated from the cross-platform by heavy reinforced concrete arches (37). The roofing of the train-sheds, designed by the engineers Eilers and Karig, mirrors the outline of these concrete arches with its steel 3-hinge ribs. As is the case with St Pancras, it is impossible to guess the shape of the train-shed at Leipzig Hauptbahnhof by studying the shape of the frontage block. The powerful and monolithically clear outlines of the station have encouraged the view that Leipzig is the last great station of the nineteenth century and, at the same time, the first of the twentieth century. It looks backwards in the neo-Baroque curves of its outline, but adopts a decidedly forward-looking stance in its choice of reinforced concrete, which at the period in question was a comparatively new building material. Extensively damaged in 1943 and 1944, the station was restored in the period up to 1960: its historical form was respected, although there is now less light in the train-sheds than there was previously (39, 40/41). This grandiose station has at all times served the city's needs admirably, and shows no sign of failing to handle the volume of traffic with which it continues to deal.

46   *Leipzig, Bayrischer Bahnhof*

One of the first long-distance routes on the continent of Europe ended at Leipzig's Bayrischer Bahnhof, built in 1842. Following the recommendations of Friedrich List, a tireless advocate of railways, the track ran from Leipzig to Nuremberg, via Reichenbach, Plauen and Hof. The line is notable above all for the Götzschtal Viaduct, the world's largest brick bridge, built in 1845-1851 and now preserved as an ancient monument. Also worth noting are the line's numerous technical systems which had never before been put to practical use, including electromagnetic safety devices invented in 1867. The Leipzig architect Eduard Poetzsch was responsible for the entire architectural and technical layout of the Bayrischer Bahnhof, which he designed as a fitting reflection of the line's importance. The surviving arch with its four openings forming the end wall of the former train-shed is one of the last buildings of this type to have been preserved. Two of the four openings were used for departures and arrivals, the third for engines and the fourth was a relief line. The left-hand tower housed the guardroom, while the right-hand tower gave access to the clock chamber. Even today the triumphal arch architecture of this station, which is otherwise badly damaged, gives a lively impression of the sense of pride which its nineteenth-century contemporaries must have felt for the new means of rapid locomotion. The Bayrischer Bahnhof is now used only for local traffic or else to take some of the load from the Hauptbahnhof when trade fairs are held in the city. Work is currently in hand to make the building safer, thus encouraging hopes that long-cherished plans for the establishment of a transport museum on the site may one day be realised.

47   Berlin, Anhalter Bahnhof

Having survived the Second World War, in spite of serious bomb damage, Berlin's Anhalter Bahnhof, the city's 'gateway to the south' and the largest and most popular of all Berlin's railway stations, having been temporarily reopened between 1946 and 1952, was finally torn down in the winter of 1959 on orders from the District Office of Kreuzberg. It took two years for the building to be demolished with the exception of a small pile of rubble for which it was no longer possible to feel any emotion and which now serves as a plinth for the battered allegorical figures of 'Day and Night'. These figures had once crowned the portico in front of Franz Schwechten's mighty row of arcade windows, looking out on to the Askanischer Platz and providing a fitting end wall for the third-biggest train-shed in Europe. The opposite end of the shed consisted of three great round arches, above which a further row of arcade windows could be seen. These two end walls were linked by a sickle-girder or arched lattice truss roof, designed by the thirty-year-old Franz Schwechten and modelled on Schwedler's new type of 3-hinge arch construction. Architectural critics of the last hundred years are all in agreement that Schwechten's station, completed in 1880, successfully met the challenge which station design now had to face. The end wall of the shed was regarded as an organic extension 'which is not a mask but a characterful face'.

48   Berlin, Hamburger Bahnhof

Leipzig's Bayrischer Bahnhof and Berlin's Hamburger Bahnhof both date from the same period and reveal the same basic outlook. The latter escaped destruction during the Second World War, no doubt because it was by then no longer being used for transport purposes, having been converted into a museum in 1906. Unlike Leipzig, Berlin's Hamburger Bahnhof, roused from its slumbers when the West Berlin Senate took over control of all the railway properties of the former Reich, still has a train-shed, although no trains have ever used it. It was erected for the opening of the Transport and Building Museum in 1906. The original train-shed had been removed in 1893 following the nationalization of the Hamburg Railway in 1884, after which date trains were diverted to the adjoining Lehrter Bahnhof. The new museum was opened on 14 December 1906 by the Kaiser Wilhelm II himself. It housed various examples of railway architecture, including a section devoted to hydraulic engineering and one to building construction. One aspect which appeared progressive in 1906 was the principle of presenting working models of many of the exhibits, an idea encouraged by the aim of the museum to serve educational ends as well as providing examples of prototype designs. It is to be hoped that, under the expert supervision of the new Berlin Museum of Transport and Technology, the Hamburger Bahnhof will be maintained and made accessible to the general public, for not only did it survive both the new building wave of second-generation stations around 1860 and the Second World War, but it contains a unique collection of exhibits and is a monument to the early history of transport.

49, 50, 51, 52/53   Frankfurt-am-Main, Hauptbahnhof

Frankfurt's Hauptbahnhof gives the impression of being an early design for Leipzig's Hauptbahnhof, which postdates it by over thirty years. Several train-sheds abut on a cross-platform which has exits at either side and in front of which is a frontage block divided into several sections. Frankfurt, however, has only one vestibule, whose roof is a continuation both in shape and direction of the central train-shed roof. There were originally three sheds with six lines each, corresponding to the originally adjoining stations of the three companies which were amalgamated to form the Hessische Ludwigsbahn and Prussian State Railway. The three sheds together cover an area of 186 metres by 168 metres. The tapered roof-ribs end in richly elaborate neck bearings at platform level and give a sense of structure to the whole vast space. The spandrels contain circular motifs with tendril-like arabesques (53), which, together with the lattice work structure of the ribs, produce an image of lively complexity (51). The individual train-sheds are closed off at their far end by low glass aprons (50). It was in 1880 that a competition was held to provide designs for a new station in Frankfurt; it attracted entries from most of the leading architects of the day and was won by Georg P. H. Eggert. Following suggestions made by J. W. Schwedler, however, the construction of the train-sheds was modified to incorporate his own system of 3-hinge arches. The Oberhausener Gutehoffnungshütte was awarded the contract to build the sheds and employed a technique of industrialized building which involved, where possible, assembling and riveting the halves of the ribs in the foundry and then transporting them by rail to the construction site. They were then fixed in position using mobile scaffolding, a process which took two years to complete. The last tracks were laid during the night of 17/18 August 1888, and the following morning at 04.47 – five years after the building had been started – the first train drew into Frankfurt's new station from the direction of Hamburg. The station assumed its present outline (49) in 1924 with the addition of two sheds on either wing, replacing the administrative blocks demolished in 1912.

54, 55 Bremen, Hauptbahnhof

The frontage of Bremen's Hauptbahnhof is brought to life by the warm colours of the bricks used in its construction. Six bonded rows of 'reddish leather-coloured' bricks are each followed by two rows of dark-red face bricks which, taken together with the terracotta decorative tiles, produces a colourful impression, giving the façade its striking orange tint (54). Chronologically, Bremen Station is one of a series of large-scale projects taken in hand following the gradual nationalization of Germany's individual railway companies. As in other towns, Bremen's new station, built between 1886 and 1891, replaced more than one older building, in this case two stations, belonging to the Hanover Company and the Cologne-Minden Company. The latter had begun discussing plans for a new station with Bremen in 1872. Provision was made, as in Leipzig, for the station complex to contain separate areas for Bremen and Cologne-Minden. Following the nationalization programme of 1879 and a state treaty of 1883, plans for the new station were taken a stage further by the directors of the Prussian Railway in Hanover. A typical feature of railway planning at this period was the idea of raised tracks running through the town, a measure which often proved more expensive in terms of building time and costs than the station building itself. The directors in Hanover commissioned the architect Hubert Stier to design the new station for Bremen, while the train-shed, built on the Müller-Breslau system, was contracted out to Dortmunder Union AG. The most striking individual feature of this through station is the use of a shed-like structure as part of the frontage block. In a terminus like Frankfurt the frontage block can be an extension to the actual train-shed. At Bremen this is not possible, since the front is parallel with the tracks, but the design makes it equally clear that here too we are confronted by a railway station. The profile of the vast train-shed roof with its concave 'saddles' made it possible for the eaves to be at a constant height, a further feature which underlines the unity of the overall design (55). For constructional reasons the massive tapering towers which flank the train-shed are built of concrete

56/57 Cologne, Hauptbahnhof

The site of Cologne's new main-line station, built between 1888 and 1894, was determined by the location of the old 'Central Passenger Station' of 1859, whose site had in turn been fixed by the first permanent Rhine bridge, completed in the same year and referred to by Cologne's inhabitants as 'the mousetrap' on account of its box-like appearance. The official name for it was the Dombrücke or Cathedral Bridge, since King Friedrich Wilhelm IV, an ardent supporter of the cathedral's building programme, had ended the long debate as to the precise siting of the bridge by letting it be known that His Majesty desired the bridge

to be aligned with the chancel of the cathedral, a decree which caused the railway no slight problems since it involved laying the tracks on a curve. However, when the new station was being planned, it was decided not to circumvent this disadvantage by shifting the site of the station. As a result Georg Frantzen's vestibule and the 2-hinge arched train-shed, built by the Dortmund Union AG to designs by the state railway administration, retained their existing site immediately north of the cathedral. The present state of Cologne Hauptbahnhof is well characterized by the commemorative stone in the entrance hall: 'Vestibule of Cologne Hauptbahnhof built in 1859, reconstructed in 1892, destroyed in 1944, rebuilt in 1957'. Like the Anhalter Bahnhof, Cologne Station had survived the air attacks of Second World War bombers in a form which could easily have been reconstructed. The post-war period, however, lacked any real understanding of the architectural achievements of the past, with the result that the train-shed is the only part of the 1894 station which has been fortunate enough to survive. Unlike other large train-sheds of the period, the one at Cologne is glazed over large areas, and its dimensions of 255 metres by 92 metres make it one of the most impressive buildings of its kind in West Germany. The current restoration of the station by the Deutsche Bundesbahn is being undertaken using the original materials of glass and iron. It is to be hoped that it will lead to a long-term preservation of the shed in as unchanged a form as possible, particularly since its present condition already represents a simplification of the more ornate shed of earlier days.

58, 59 Hamburg, Dammtor Bahnhof

Two new stations opened in Hamburg in 1903, at Sternschanze and Dammthor. Both were the work of the same architect and engineer, respectively Schwartz and Merlig. The vestibules at both stations are situated on the ground floor (58), above which soars a single-span steel trussed shed, 34 metres in width, covering four rails and two platforms. One unusual feature here is the form of lighting: in addition to the daylight entering through the glass screen at the far end of the shed, the interior was also lit by large windows in the sides of the building (59). The roof was not glazed.

60 Hamburg, Hauptbahnhof

The same iron-built structure which had been seen at the Paris Exhibition of 1889 and which was to displace St Pancras as the largest building of its kind in the world served as a model for Hamburg's Hauptbahnhof, begun in 1903. A competition was held in 1900 to find suitable designs and the partnership of Reinhardt and Süssenguth emerged as winners. Tenders for building the train-shed were invited in 1902, and awarded to the Düsseldorf firm of Brückenbau Flender AG. Together with Hein

Lehmann and August Klönne, they assembed the building materials supplied by Thyssen AG of Mülheim/Ruhr. The 'ship's bottom profile' of this structurally lucid and economically designed shed is a delightful reminder of Hamburg's position as a port, affording an example of what for the period was a novel type of construction and use of space. The result was the widest single-span shed on the continent. Also new was the idea of using the cross-platform as a bridge spanning the individual platforms of this through station, which are situated at a lower level and buttressed by a series of smaller vaults perpendicular to the main shed. According to the 1902 designs, the vestibule was intended to be decorated with Art Nouveau motifs which would have complemented the lucidity of the iron structure. The idea provoked strong opposition from Kaiser Wilhelm II, who is reported to have described the suggestion as 'simply dreadful' and demanded a design modelled on Hamburg's town-hall. A modified version was produced, inspired by the 'German Renaissance', although the question of cost offered a welcome opportunity to make a number of alterations in the direction of greater simplicity of design.

61, 63, 64, 65, 66   *Helsinki, Rautatieasema Järnvägsstation*

The new century produced a new type of station building: towers began to play an increasing role, the train-shed became less visually striking externally than the frontage block, which more and more frequently included huge portico arches. A particularly picturesque and graphic representative of this type is the main station in Helsinki, completed by Eliel Saarinen in 1914 (66). The lateral positioning of the clock tower (64) disguises the fact that the overall layout of this terminus is symmetrical, having the form of a letter 'U' centred round the huge round-arched window of the concourse building (65). The whole structure is strikingly ponderous and massive, though what is even more striking are the four monumental figures on the main façade, which take on an almost ghost-like character at night with enormous globe-shaped lamps in their out-stretched hands. Their Nordic mythical appearance is a good example of the national romantic style which was fashionable in the years leading up to the First World War (63, 66).

67, 69, 70, 71, 72   *Genoa, Stazione Piazza Principe*

The unification of Italy brought with it a framework and an incentive to build a whole new series of triumphal station buildings in Turin, Trieste, Genoa, Milan, Rome and Naples, and the Renaissance style of architecture inevitably presented itself as a suitable expression of the nation's rebirth. In Genoa, Italy's most important trading port and a leading industrial centre, the site of the main station, formerly known as the Stazione Occidentale, lies in the Piazza Acquaverde between two

hills overlooking the inner harbour. The frontage block of the station, which dates from 1860, takes up two sides of the piazza. The two wings, which originally both ended in triumphal arches, meet at right angles in the corner of the square to form a central booking hall (70), a successful solution both architecturally and in terms of local town planning. As with many other Italian stations, the outer platforms are individually roofed (67), each roof section being edged with broad, richly ornamented sheets of metal. The roof of the vestibule is glazed, in the manner of an arcade, the two halves of the roof meeting at the axial booking hall (69, 72). The rooms which abut on the vestibule (71) are lavishly decorated in marble and ornamental plasterwork.

73, 74, 75   *Turin, Stazione Porta Nuova*

The concourse of Turin's Stazione di Porta Nuova of 1866-1868 owes its present appearance to the modernization programme carried out in 1954 (73). The building, which covers a wide area, has arcades on the ground floor, while the first-floor façade is an almost unbroken row of round-arched windows. The arcades of the ground floor are repeated in the central part of the building, whose upper section follows the shape of the train-shed (75). This wall is similarly delimited by round arches and largely articulated by windows, with the result that at night the façade looks down on the Piazza Carlo Felice like some huge semicircle, lit from behind by the lights of the train-shed. The shed as originally designed by the engineer Carlo Ceppi was not glazed at its far end. It has now been converted into a large booking hall, while the platforms for the twenty tracks have been pushed back behind an equally new, glazed concourse.

76, 77, 78/79, 80, 81, 82/83, 84   *Milan, Stazione Centrale*

Milan's main station was planned at about the same time as Leipzig's Hauptbahnhof: it surpasses the 66,000 square metres surface area of this second-largest of European stations by a tenth. Milan is the last major station in Europe to have a steel-built train-shed (78/79); of the five individual roofs, one has a span of 73 metres, two of 45, and two of 12 metres each. As in Turin, the end of the huge shed is open, so that from this side one has the feeling of looking into a vast tunnel (76). On turning round, the observer is confronted by a confusion of tracks and, beyond them, the strict symmetry of water-towers, workshops and signal boxes (72), an arrangement which is typical of many large stations. The competition held to produce designs for a new station in Milan was won by Ulisse Stacchini, and work began on the building in 1906, only to be interrupted by the First World War. Work was subsequently resumed on the building in 1923, and the station was completed in 1931. Its larger-than-life monumentality, however, was added in the final stages of building: planned before the days of Mussolini, the station kept pace with the growth of Fascism and acquired an increasingly triumphal grandeur (80, 81), although its style of architecture was not altogether typical of the period, as is clear from the slightly later station of Santa Maria Novella in Florence. The traveller in Milan has to negotiate an enormous flight of stairs between the concourse and the cross-platform: prior to doing so, he will have had to pass through the pretentious *porte cochère*, before his exhausting route march finally brings him within sight of the platforms themselves. Milan is the dinosaur among nineteenth-century stations, among whose number we are entitled to place it by virtue not of its date of building but its style of architecture. Not even the most monumental of stations in the New World can compete with it. It requires a Mediterranean outlook on life to create a corner of human activity in this colossus of a building, and that corner is the bar above one of the flights of stairs leading to the booking hall (84).

85, 88 *Barcelona, Estaçion de Francia*

Barcelona's Termino Station, also known as the Estaçion de Francia, was completed after the end of the First World War. It is the largest station of any of the Catalan cities. The traveller enters the domed vestibule by one of three large glazed openings, and from there proceeds into the two-bay train-shed (85) which, as in Brighton (15) and York (18, 19), is slightly curved. From the inside of the shed (88) it is possible to see the longitudinal walls of the buildings which run along the sides of the shed.

87 *Madrid, Atocha*

The majority of Spanish towns have retained the separate stations which date back to the days of the country's private rail companies. Barcelona has four, Bilboa six and Madrid a further three stations, Madrid's North Station being linked to the other termini. Atocha is the starting point for the lines heading south and east. The frontage block is at ground level, its central gable catching the eye with its glass screen: above it, and showing the influence of French models, soars the glazed gable wall of the train-shed.

89 *Barcelona, Estaçion del Norte*

A second terminus in Barcelona is the Estaçion del Norte in the Plaza Cataluña. Its ticket counter remains completely unaltered, like the one at Toledo: both reflect the conservative style which flourished south of the Pyrenees and which is responsible for the somewhat provincial blend of neo-Rococo and Art Nouveau, of which a good example is the barrier in front of the steel-built, glazed-off train-shed of the Estaçion del Norte.

90, 91 *Valencia, Estaçion del Norte*

French influence is also evident in the station at Valencia, Spain's third-largest city with 1.8 million inhabitants. The architect in this case, however, has made concessions to the station's geographical position on Spain's torrid east coast, in that light enters the train-shed not through an extensively glazed roof but through a skylight at the apex of the roof and through the perpendicular fenestration of the side walls. The concourse acquires a hint of foreign climes thanks to the polyglot greetings to travellers inlaid in mosaic (91). Mosaic is also used in the booking hall, where the name of the station 'Norte' appears beside each of the ticket windows. Above each of the Art Nouveau lamps on the columns in this hall, the capital decoration includes a three-dimensional representation of an orange (91), the chief export product of the province of Valencia.

92 *Seville, Estaçion de Huelva*

Only when we reach the southernmost stations of the Iberian peninsula does Moorish influence become apparent and produce a characteristically Spanish type of historical style. The Estaçion de Huelva in Seville's Plaza de Armas is a strikingly coherent example of this stylistic principle, applied consistently both to the flanking pavilions of the main façade and to the central section and gable wall of the train-shed. Conservative in its basic outline, the Seville terminus also shows Moorish influence in the horseshoe arches of its windows and doorways, in the ziggurats crowning the two pavilions and in the sheet-iron frieze bordering the glazed frontage of the building, as well as in the shape of the wall and door surfaces.

93, 94 *Toledo*

The foregoing remarks apply with even greater force to Toledo Station in central Spain. In outline, the prominent five-arched booking hall, the two wings and the flanking clock tower, with a richly decorated chimney to act as a counterbalance, make up a station of thoroughly conventional stamp. The historicist Moorish decorations, applied both to the exterior (93) and the interior and still intact today, give the building the exotic charm of some fairy-tale palace from the Thousand and One Nights. The traveller enters the station through a portico decorated with lanterns and emerges into a lofty, cool hall into which daylight filters through stained-glass windows. Here he is confronted by the confusingly intricate carvings of the booking hall windows, from which he might far rather expect to see the veiled features of a harem beauty bending towards him than the prosaically capped head of a booking hall clerk. Beneath the heavy coffered ceiling with its huge pendant candelabra, the traveller may linger a while in silent, untroubled contemplation of this fine example of historicism in Hispanic architecture, while outside the silver-gleaming express train pulls out of the station on its way to Madrid.

95, 97 *Lisbon, Estação do Rossio*

The frontage block of Lisbon's Estação Central (often referred to simply as the Rossio, after the square where it is built) takes us back to a different period of architectural history. In the hustle and bustle of the busy square, situated at the end of the city's magnificent Avenida de Liberdade, the three-storey frontage of the station appears at first sight to give no indication that behind it lies one of Lisbon's four stations, the more so since the ground beyond the building begins almost immediately to slope upwards. For that reason trains disappear into a tunnel the moment they leave the station's iron-built, saddleback train-shed. If, however, one looks more closely at the front of the building, its two coupled horseshoe doorways reveal its public purpose. It owes its remarkable appearance to the stylistic forms of Manueline, a style between late Gothic and early Renaissance exclusive to Portugal and typified by elements such as chains, ropes and ships' wheels, the insignia of a nation which, on the threshold of the modern era, had been the first to commit its destiny to shipping and to trade with the Indies. The Estação do Rossio was designed in 1890 by the architect José Luis Monteiro for the Companhia Real dos Caminhos de Ferro Portugueses. Apart from the façade already mentioned, the station's other notable feature is the medallions on the side walls of the train-shed, depicting regional produce.

98, 99, 100 *Porto, Estação de São Bento*

Far removed from the influence of manuelist art is the U-shaped terminus of São Bento at Porto in northern Portugal. Although planned at the end of the nineteenth century, it was not built until 1916. Neo-Baroque in form, the building might at first sight almost give the impression of being a town mansion, were it not for the clocks on the tower-like corner projections facing the street. As in Lisbon, trains disappear into a tunnel immediately after leaving the train-shed at Porto. An impressive feature here is the concourse, lit by seven tall round-arched windows. Jorge Colaco designed the large tile pictures in the concourse in 1914, representing scenes from rural life and Portuguese history, but also paying homage to the railway era with their depiction of a locomotive and telegraph masts. The same motif is inscribed on the dial of a clock which, like the station's handbell, indicates the increasing importance of timekeeping in an age of growing industrialization (98).

103, 104, 105 *Limoges, Gare de Limoges-Bénédictins*

The reinforced concrete structure at Limoges-Bénédictins, designed by the architect Roger Gonthier for the Compagnie du Paris-Orléans and built between 1924 and 1929, was intended to draw attention to the town's importance as the centre of France's porcelain industry; but all who have seen the building are tempted to compare it, rather, to the layout of a mosque, a comparison encouraged by the station's semicircular cupola and minaret-like clock tower (104). The sculptor Henri Varenne later created two allegorical female figures for the south front, symbolizing the porcelain industry: agriculture and industry appear in the portico spandrels (105), and the pictorial cycle is completed by female figures in the four corners of the concourse, representing the four regions through which the railway passes, Limousin, Touraine, Brittany and Gascony (103). A more modern feature, and one which is therefore more in keeping with the period when the station was built, are the stained-glass windows made by the Limoges artist Francis Chigot.

106 *Nice*

The sumptuous building of the Gare du Sud in Nice was built in 1892 as the terminus of the line from the surrounding area of the Var and Durance départements. Unlike the other stations along the line, which were conventional in design and materials, this one had architectural aspirations: 'a monumental edifice in a rather indeterminate style', as one critic commented. The building itself is now disused and in danger of falling into decay, though the line is still operating. The Baroque forms of its pavilions are matched by the luxuriant decoration of the ironwork on the twin train-sheds. At the end of the canopies, swags of fruit link the tie-rods of the arches to a lion's head surmounted by a palmette.

107 *Tours*

The station at Tours, designed by Victor Laloux and built between 1895 and 1898, stands within the tradition of main-line French stations of the second half of the nineteenth century. Whereas arched train-sheds had been typical of English and, later, German stations of the time, French sheds, with few exceptions, had saddleback roofs, necessitated by the French predilection for the so-called Polonceau truss. The façade of Tours station reveals this form with transparent clarity. The twin-arched portals form the focal point of the frontage block, clearly separated from each other and from the flanking corner buildings by massive columns. Here, too, on the main line between Paris and Bordeaux, the French love of allegorical decoration finds abundant expression: huge figures have usurped the place of the station clock, which had once been an important architectural feature and which has here been relegated to the lower regions of the space between the two train-sheds.

108, 109 *Paris, Gare du Nord*

The second station at the Gare du Nord in Paris was designed by Jacques Ignace Hittorf and built between 1861 and 1865. The train-shed was the work of François Léonce Reynaud, its proportions clearly reflected in the spacious façade which here, too, draws on the allegorical figure of womankind to personify the station's destinations (108). Inside the building the tall, narrow iron columns in no way impair the magnificent impression of spaciousness created by the 74-metre wide shed, although equally wide sheds in Great Britain create a more harmonious effect with the curving lines of their roofs, the more so in that there is a closer and more convincing correspondence in British stations between the round-arched windows of the frontage block and the shape of the train-shed behind.

101, 110, 111, 112 *Paris, Gare de Lyon*

The connection between the Paris Exhibition of 1900 and the rebuilding of the Gare de Lyon for the Paris-Lyon-Mediterranean Line (PLM) was not only a chronological one: its architect, Denis-Marius Toudoire, was also responsible for the Palais des Manufactures Nationales. The Gare de Lyon, with its lateral clock tower reminiscent of the station at Limoges (101), proclaims, in its own way, the belief in technological progress which was characteristic of the turn of the century. Allegories of sea-travel, steam, mechanical engineering and electricity, together with prosperity, industry, trade and agriculture, make up the optimistic programme which the façade presents (110). In spite of all this, the station was technologically behind the times. A thoroughly old-fashioned-looking traverser was installed in the two-bay steel-built train-shed to transfer the carriages from one rail to another. Steps played an important part in the development of the site, since the station is situated at a higher level than the surrounding area (112).

113 *Paris, Gare St Lazare*

The first of France's western railways to be nationalized, apart from the Gare Montparnasse and the Gare des Invalides, was the Gare St-Lazare on the right bank of the Seine. The station was repeatedly rebuilt, and in 1886-1889 a new concourse was added by Gustave Lisch and positioned in front of the various existing sheds. Here, too, we find a saddleback roof typical of most of Paris's railway stations.

114, 115, 116 *Paris, Gare de l'Est*

The most striking feature of the Gare de l'Est is the way in which the end of the train-shed pierces the façade with an enormous arched window: in this way, the shed, which is of an unusual construction for Paris stations, imposes its character and shape on the architecture of the main frontage block. If we compare the Gare de l'Est with London's King's Cross (13), we see the same composition of their respective elements,

but the former is more harmonious and more perfectly, decoratively balanced. When the station was built by Duquesney between 1847 and 1852, contemporaries were in little doubt that it was the finest in the world. The iron-built shed, more than 100 metres long, was three storeys high on its longer sides, but at the front it was limited to a single storey, so that the great gable of the shed would be clearly visible from the Boulevard de Strasbourg. The Grande Cour in front of the façade is an enclosed courtyard of impressive dimensions. The ideal prerequisite of the time, namely that the clearly defined dominant feature should be flanked by subordinate elements, had been met. Later modifications have diluted the original conception but have not completely destroyed it.

117, 119, 120/121, 122 *Antwerp, Centraal Station*

When plans were drawn up in the 1890s for the rebuilding of Antwerp's sixth district, it was resolved to build a new main-line station, a building which was to become one of the most impressive of all Belgium's stations. The vast iron shed, started in 1895, was 185 metres long and 44 metres at its highest point (117, 120/121). The building of the shed took three years to complete, and in June 1898 the first train drew out of the station, which as yet lacked a concourse. The Bruges architect Louis de la Censerie designed the neo-Baroque head-building in 1897. Begun in 1900, it was completed five years later and formed a monumental finish to the magnificent Avenue de Keyser. No fewer than ten towers surround the huge dome, which the Ministry of Railways hoped would finally give Antwerp a station commensurate with its reputation as a centre of art. Two lantern-crowned octagonal towers flank the façade in which the motif of a large semicircular window twice appears (122). In modified form this is also the view overlooking the Avenue de Keyser. There is not a single square metre either inside or outside the vast concourse which is not decorated; clocks, as always, play an important part (119). All in all, Antwerp Centraal Station is a worthy monument to a country which was the first on the continent to control a close-woven network of railways.

125, 126, 127 *Amsterdam, Centraal Station*

When Amsterdam Centraal Station was rebuilt between 1881 and 1889, the old shed, then only twenty years old, was torn down to make way for a two-bay barrel-roofed shed behind a new frontage block designed by the architect of the Rijksmuseum, Petrus Cuypers. Indebted in style to the Dutch Renaissance, it became the most elaborately decorated station building in the whole of the Netherlands. Situated on the axis of the Damrak, one of the city's main arteries, the building site had first to be reclaimed from the waters of Amsterdam harbour. The station still stands on its own island. In 1922, a new double shed was built, measuring 350 metres long by 34 metres wide (126, 127); seen in lateral elevation, its end walls appear totally unconnected with the frontage block. The station exercised a decisive influence on the development of the Damrak. Countless hotels and the city's new stock exchange have usurped the site of the old warehouses on the quayside. A spectacular example of interior design is provided by the station's royal waiting room, which also displays its presence externally in the royal coats of arms of Willem II and Queen Emma on the right-hand section of the outer façade. A flight of stairs (125) leads up to the waiting room, a room for the royal attendants and the lavatories for the royal suite. The walls are partly clad in marble and partly painted with brick motifs, conjuring up an age when the rules of the social hierarchy, played an essential role in influencing the design of station concourses.

123, 128, 129, 130, 131, 132 *Haarlem*
When a new station was built in Haarlem in 1908, it was restricted exclusively to passenger traffic in an attempt to improve conditions in the inner city. The station complex is dominated by the train-shed (129), designed by the engineer Werker and clearly visible from all sides. An additional platform was added to the north of the shed in 1953. One notable feature of this station, which is heavily influenced by Art Nouveau, are the buildings on the island platform inside the train-shed, containing offices (128). The waiting rooms (130), offices (131) and sides of the shed are all provided with wooden supports. E. Cuypers designed the numerous tile motifs (128, 130) which the station contains, a tradition revived on the occasion of the celebrations held to mark the centenary of the Dutch Railways (123). Even the guild of porters, by now an almost extinct species, donated a tile to decorate the station. The motif of a man carrying suitcases with stickers from large international hotels may help today's traveller to recreate the vision of a century in which rail travel first opened up the world for many people – a world which shrank in size as the new technological potential grew and in which remote distances suddenly came within reach.